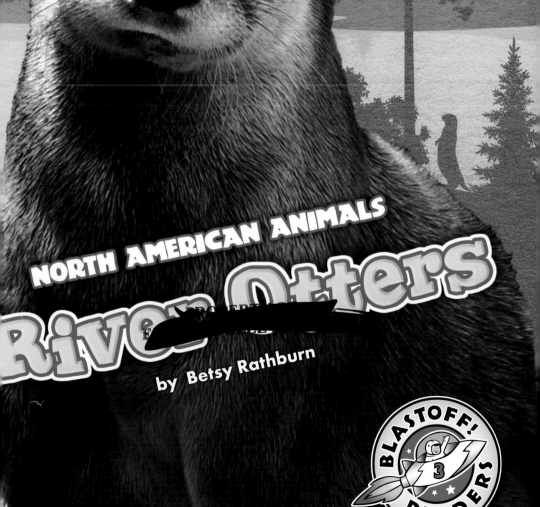

NORTH AMERICAN ANIMALS

River Otters

by Betsy Rathburn

BLASTOFF!
3
READERS

BELLWETHER MEDIA • MINNEAPOLIS, MN

Note to Librarians, Teachers, and Parents:

Blastoff! Readers are carefully developed by literacy experts and combine standards-based content with developmentally appropriate text.

Level 1 provides the most support through repetition of high-frequency words, light text, predictable sentence patterns, and strong visual support.

Level 2 offers early readers a bit more challenge through varied simple sentences, increased text load, and less repetition of high-frequency words.

Level 3 advances early-fluent readers toward fluency through increased text and concept load, less reliance on visuals, longer sentences, and more literary language.

Level 4 builds reading stamina by providing more text per page, increased use of punctuation, greater variation in sentence patterns, and increasingly challenging vocabulary.

Level 5 encourages children to move from "learning to read" to "reading to learn" by providing even more text, varied writing styles, and less familiar topics.

Whichever book is right for your reader, Blastoff! Readers are the perfect books to build confidence and encourage a love of reading that will last a lifetime!

This edition first published in 2018 by Bellwether Media, Inc.

No part of this publication may be reproduced in whole or in part without written permission of the publisher. For information regarding permission, write to Bellwether Media, Inc., Attention: Permissions Department, 5357 Penn Avenue South, Minneapolis, MN 55419.

Library of Congress Cataloging-in-Publication Data

Names: Rathburn, Betsy, author.
Title: River Otters / by Betsy Rathburn.
Other titles: Blastoff! Readers. 3, North American Animals.
Description: Minneapolis, MN : Bellwether Media, Inc., [2018] | Series: Blastoff! Readers: North American Animals |
    Audience: Ages 5-8. | Audience: K to Grade 3. | Includes bibliographical references and index.
Identifiers: LCCN 2017028796 | ISBN 9781626177307 (hardcover : alk. paper) | ISBN 9781681034713 (ebook)
Subjects: LCSH: Otters–Juvenile literature.
Classification: LCC QL737.C25 R38 2018 | DDC 599.769/2–dc23
LC record available at https://lccn.loc.gov/2017028796

Editor: Rebecca Sabelko   Designer: Josh Brink

Printed in the United States of America, North Mankato, MN.

Table of Contents

What Are River Otters?

River otters are water-loving **mammals**. They are usually found in rivers, **marshes**, and **swamps**.

N
W   E
S

North American
river otter range =

conservation status: least concern

Extinct

Extinct in
the Wild

Critically
Endangered

Endangered

Vulnerable

Near
Threatened

Least
Concern

North American river otters live
throughout the United States and
Canada. **Neotropical** river otters
are found from Mexico to Panama.

River otters live in **dens**.
They make these in hollow
logs and riverbanks.

They also make dens from the **burrows** of other animals. These usually have underwater entrances that lead to nests lined with grass and leaves.

Made for the Water

River otters spend most of their time in water. They use their long, flat tails to help them swim.

Identify a River Otter

thick tail

short legs

webbed feet

Webbed feet help river otters paddle quickly. These animals can swim about 6 miles (9.7 kilometers) per hour!

River otters have flat heads and small ears. They can close their ears and noses to keep water out.

Their bodies are covered in thick brown fur. This **waterproof** fur helps river otters stay warm and dry in cold water.

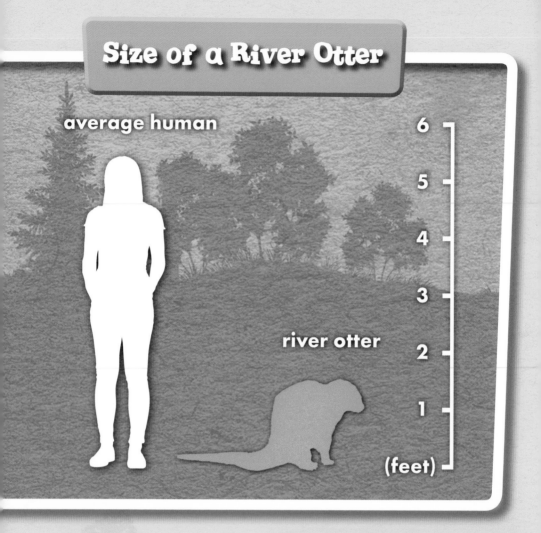

Size of a River Otter

average human

river otter

6
5
4
3
2
1

(feet)

Adult river otters are about 3 feet (0.9 meters) to 4 feet (1.2 meters) long. Their tails can be more than 1 foot (0.3 meters) long!

The otters can weigh up to 30 pounds (13.6 kilograms).

River otters are **carnivores**. These skilled swimmers eat mostly fish.

crayfish

green frogs

zebra mussels

painted turtles

muskrats

largemouth bass

Other favorite foods are crabs, crayfish, and mussels. Sometimes, they eat insects and small mammals.

River otters have few **predators** in water. They are mainly **prey** to alligators.

neotropical
river otter

Animals to Avoid

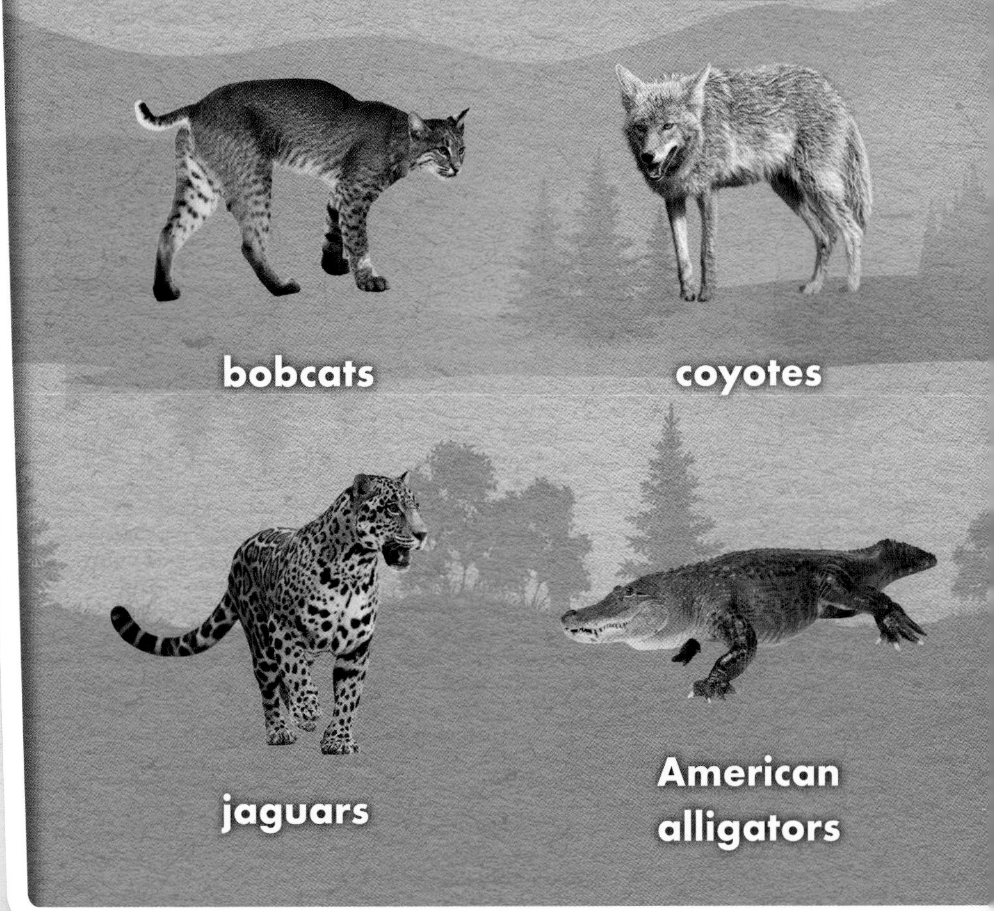

bobcats

coyotes

jaguars

American alligators

Common land predators include coyotes and bobcats. In Mexico and Central America, river otters must avoid prowling jaguars.

Playful Pups

Every winter or spring, female river otters have up to six **pups**. In about two months, the pups go outside. There, they spend most of their time playing near the den.

Baby Facts

Name for babies:	pups
Size of litter:	1 to 6 pups
Length of pregnancy:	60 to 63 days
Time spent with mom:	about 1 year

Otter families love to play.
Pups wrestle and chase
one another. Mom may
join in, too.

They also slide down hills and splash into the water. This playtime helps them learn to hunt!

Glossary

burrows—holes or tunnels that some animals dig for homes

carnivores—animals that only eat meat

dens—sheltered places

mammals—warm-blooded animals that have backbones and feed their young milk

marshes—wetlands filled with grasses and other plants with stems

neotropical—related to the area that surrounds the south, east, and west of central Mexico

predators—animals that hunt other animals for food

prey—animals that are hunted by other animals for food

pups—baby river otters

swamps—wetlands filled with trees and other woody plants

waterproof—able to keep water from soaking through

webbed feet—feet with thin skin that connects the toes

To Learn More

AT THE LIBRARY

Lawrence, Ellen. *North American River Otter*. New York, N.Y.: Bearport Publishing, 2017.

Lynette, Rachel. *Giant River Otters*. New York, N.Y.: Bearport Publishing, 2013.

Niver, Heather M. Moore. *River Otters After Dark*. New York, N.Y.: Enslow Publishing, 2017.

ON THE WEB

Learning more about river otters is as easy as 1, 2, 3.

1. Go to www.factsurfer.com.

2. Enter "river otters" into the search box.

3. Click the "Surf" button and you will see a list of related web sites.

With factsurfer.com, finding more information is just a click away.

Index

The images in this book are reproduced through the courtesy of: Derrick Neill, front cover; Elliotte Rusty Harold, pp. 4, 12; ZUMA Press Inc/ Alamy, p. 6; Kevin Wells/ Alamy, p. 7; Steve Cordory, p. 8; Carl Olsen, p. 9 (top left); Alexandr Junek Imaging, p. 9 (top middle); trabantos, p. 9 (top right); Jan Gottwald, p. 9 (bottom); Vladimir Wrangel, p. 10; Robbie George/ Alamy, p. 11; DejaVuDesigns, p. 13; Ghost Bear, p. 14; vengerof, p. 15 (top left); Nancy Kennedy, p. 15 (top right); Vitalii Hulai, p. 15 (middle left); Gerald A. DeBoer, p. 15 (middle right); Sergey Uryadnikov, p. 15 (bottom left); StevenRussellSmithPhotos, p. 15 (bottom right); MostardiPhotography/ Alamy, p. 16; Svetlana Foote, p. 17 (top left); Cynthia Kidwell, p. 17 (top right); Anan Kaewkhammul, p. 18 (bottom left); Eric Isselee, p. 17 (bottom right); Tom & Pat Leeson/ Age Fotostock, p. 18; Laura Romin & Larry Dalton/ Alamy, p. 19; milehightraveler, p. 20; CHARLIE JAMES/ Alamy, p. 21.